W9-CPF-574

Swanfall

Swanfall

Journey of the Tundra Swans

Tom Horton
Photographs by David Harp

Walker and Company  *New York*

First published in the United States of America in 1991
by Walker Publishing Company, Inc.

Published simultaneously in Canada by Thomas Allen & Son
Canada, Limited, Markham, Ontario

Library of Congress Cataloging-in-Publication Data
Horton, Tom, 1945--
Swanfall: journey of the tundra swans / Tom Horton; photographs by David Harp.
p. cm
Summary: Text and photographs record the habits and Characteristics of a family of tundra swans while following them for a year's time.
ISBN 0-8027-8106-3 --ISBN 0-8027-8107-1 (Rein)
1. Tundra swan--Juvenile literature. [1. Tundra swan.
2. Swans.] I. Harp, David W., ill. II. Title.
QL696.A52H67 1991
598.4'1--dc20 91-15380
CIP
AC

Printed in Hong Kong

2 4 6 8 10 9 7 5 3 1

Book Design Georg Brewer

Photograph credits: pages 37 and 38 (bottom) by
Michael Wootton; pages 38 (top) and 42 by Jon Bart.

This book is dedicated to Dr. William J. L. Sladen, who taught us the possibilities of swans.

—Tom Horton and David Harp

The November sun cast long, afternoon slants across the flat sweep of Blackwater National Wildlife Refuge on the Chesapeake Bay, burnishing the marshes to rich gold and cinnamon. The light silhouetted flocks of wintering Canada geese, mallards, pintails, teal, and black ducks feeding on ponds. It glinted from brassy mounds of shelled grain, discharged into waiting trucks by harvesting machines that lumbered through the rows of corn on nearby farms. Out on the broad Chesapeake, the fishermen pulled their crab traps for the last time and readied their gear for a season of oystering.

The autumn scene seemed complete, yet something vital was still missing. A fisherman noticed his barometer falling, indicating that the golden Indian summer

weather was about to give way to something fiercer. That afternoon a message came to refuge headquarters from a remote station in North Dakota: the swans were on their way.

Since mid-September they had been gathering for this moment, streaming into the lakes and marshes of the treeless Dakota prairie, chased by advancing winter from nesting grounds that stretched from the rim of the Arctic Ocean to the Hudson Bay. By late October nearly 100,000 of the great white birds were packed into the area around Jamestown, North Dakota.

Wow-HOW-oo! Wow-HOW-oo! Their wild yodeling pierced the frosty air for miles, pure and fluid as a French horn, yet primeval as any wolf's howling. Only a windpipe that looped and stretched nearly four feet within those long necks could produce such otherworldly music.

In one corner of a shallow Dakota lake, two large adults, a male and a female, fed greedily. They extended their long necks underwater to rip up the starchy roots of the sago pondweed that carpeted the bottom. Where they could not reach quite deep enough, the swans "tipped," submerging the whole front halves of their bodies, using their webbed feet to maintain balance as they vigorously excavated the bottom.

It was the pondweed with its starchy tubers that drew the swans here. They gorged several pounds a day of the submerged vegetation. Just as a marathon runner fuels up on starches before a grueling race, so the swans were taking on board all the reserves of fat they could manage for the final, big push to the Chesapeake and the lean winter ahead.

Swans are the world's largest waterfowl and among the largest flighted birds on the globe. The pair we watch are in their tenth autumn of life, not old for swans, which may survive beyond twenty years in the wild. Their wing spans are more than seven feet, and the male weighs nearly twenty pounds, the female about two pounds less.

They are tundra swans, the fourth most numerous of the world's seven kinds of swans, and the dominant species in North America. Of all the swans, the tundras undertake the longest migration, an odyssey of up to four thousand miles, which must be completed twice each year for their species to survive.

In the adults' wake sailed a trio of slightly smaller swans, with a leaden cast to their white feathers. Their necks and heads looked as if they had been powdered with soot. These were the pair's young, or *cygnets,* hatched only a few months before and now preparing for the longest nonstop journey of their lives.

The cygnets grubbed the lake bottom for tubers but also fed on the grassy debris churned to the surface by their parents. They were joined by raucous gaggles of other hangers-on—wigeon, mallards, and coots, all of

whom fed on what the swans, with their longer reach, tore from the bottom.

November had come to the Dakotas, dusting the fields of grain and sunflowers with early snows. The swans still fed, but now they grew fidgety. Frequently the male would thrust his great neck forward, hurling a loud *wow-HOW-oo* heavenward. Massive wings and feet the size of Ping-Pong paddles flailed the lake as he gained the air with surprising speed for a bird so large, climbing briefly before splashing back down. The cygnets watched him, made high-pitched "wheeping" calls, and tested their own wings.

Ice began to rim the bigger lakes. The brilliant sun glared and winked from the hard-frozen surfaces of a thousand smaller marsh potholes. Yet the swans hung on, walking on ice solid enough to support them, almost hesitant at the knowledge that once they departed there would be no turning back, no setting down for over a thousand miles.

The ice continued to grow. The final nudge came from the storm, a fierce cold front whistling down from Canada, bound for the bay country. The winds flowing south as the norther blustered through gave the big birds the boost they needed. It was time.

As the flows of water in the river channels braiding through the northern plains grew sluggish with ice, a great river of swans, wings threshing the air with a jingly, sighing sound, began flowing high above. The tundras used to be called whistling swans. The origin of the name is not clear, but perhaps it was the musical sound made by the wind passing through the birds' feathers.

The swans did not move in a mass, like many long-distance migrators, but in small groups of loosely related families—adults and cygnets, and young adults bred in previous years who had not reached the age of taking their own mates.

On the coattails of the storm just past, they rose, necks extended, feet tucked against their hindquarters for minimum wind resistance. The big male flew at the point of one V of ten birds, his powerful wing beats breaking a trail through the air for the cygnets behind.

Through the afternoon the swans labored southward as the plains fell away behind them. Dawn tinted their breasts and underbellies a creamy, lustrous rose as Lake Erie slipped by beneath their ceaseless wing beats. The V, already flying at several thousand feet, climbed even higher to take advantage of air currents.

The pilot of a jetliner, cruising the cloud canyons at more than three miles above the earth, watched the chevron of swans arrowing across the vast, blue dome of sky. His plane suddenly seemed a clumsy instrument of flight next to these travelers. So pure and white in the unfiltered light of high altitude, they could have been a band of angels, dipped down from heaven, he thought. The pilot marveled at how birds the size and weight of Christmas turkeys could haul themselves across half of the American continent in these realms where oxygen is almost nonexistent. He snapped a salute. Good journey.

The swans pressed on. Their mastery of distance and altitude represented perfection by an evolutionary process that had been working for some 30 million years. That is the earliest date for which fossils of a waterfowl closely resembling modern-day swans have been found in the beds of prehistoric lakes in Europe.

The same long, looping windpipe that creates the unforgettable sounds of the tundra swan functions as part of a respiratory system which scours oxygen from the air far better than our own lungs. Unlike most creatures, the swans do not lower the efficiency of their lungs by exhaling after inhaling. Instead, their windpipe expels the used air, letting the lungs continuously inhale. The basic design is not unlike that of some of our most advanced jet engines.

For all their size and bulk, the tundra swans have evolved to slip through the air with surprising ease. Scientists who used wind tunnels to test flight ability in a variety of birds—from swans and eagles to ducks and geese—were astonished to find the swan was hands down the most aerodynamic. The shape of the swans, which through the ages has appealed to poets and artists for its grace and beauty, is also quite practical for getting the birds where they need to go with the least expenditure of energy.

As the morning wore on, the river of swans, now strung out in little groups for hundreds of miles, began passing over Pittsburgh, Pennsylvania, descending enough that their *wow-HOW-oo*ing drifted to earth. One year, a flock was forced down on the Allegheny River by fog, and the hubbub of the swans' voices brought police swarming, sure that a horrible riot was in progress.

On this day, as it did everywhere, the swansound skirling down from the sky like the baying of distant hounds set dogs barking in backyards. It caused people in the city streets to pause and look skyward, held for a moment by a feeling so old and deep they could not explain it much better than the dogs could their barking.

Perhaps in ancient times, when humans were still nomads pursuing food and shelter wherever nature provided it, the passage of the swans signaled that it was time to be moving south. We no longer need to do that, of course. The sounds of the swans no longer have survival value for us. But we still find them thrilling.

The vee of swans with the adults and their three cygnets had been aloft close to twenty hours, averaging nearly fifty miles an hour. The Chesapeake lay before them, a great, inviting bay stretching up more than two hundred miles from the ocean at Norfolk, Virginia, past Baltimore, Maryland, almost to Pennsylvania's southern border. Its crinkly, ragged shoreline—which would be more than eight thousand miles long if it were straightened out—held thousands of protected coves where the swans could rest and feed throughout the winter.

The region's first big cold front whipped the bay's shallow waters to whitecaps and set the marshes rippling and arching beneath the wind's stroking. At Blackwater Refuge, nearly a full day after the message of lift-off from North Dakota, the glimmering strings of swans began their grateful descent.

Floating at such height that they appeared to flicker in the light of afternoon, the birds began a balletlike series of glides and "whiffles," tilting from side to side to lose altitude by spilling the buoying air from their wings. Moving ever lower, yelping and halloooing, the swans mastered the buffeting wind as if carving their descent from some firmer, more stable substance than thin air.

As the big birds approached touch down, their aerodynamic lines began to reshape, sinuous and fluid as those of the reptiles from which they descended

long ago. Their necks arched, arched, arched some more. Breasts swelled. Big paddlefeet swung smoothly down to brake their forward motion. Wings cupped, curved, back-paddled the air—a gentle *plishhhh* of water parting to buoy and embrace the tired traveler. The odyssey of the tundra swan was complete for another season.

For the next few days, more and more of the swans' fellows spilled into the bay, and into similar coastal environments as far south as the Carolinas. The swans at first did little but rest and sleep, floating with long necks coiled across their backs, bills tucked into a wing. Against the dark marsh banks of Chesapeake coves, they looked from a distance like snowbanks, or ice floes clumped together.

From his home on a creek that fed the bay, a man watched the return of the tundra swans with special gladness in his heart. He is a world-famous scientist who studies birds, an ornithologist, and his interests have taken him from penguins in the Antarctic to snow

geese in Siberia. Of all the birds, the swans are among his most favorite. In his native Britain, they have a lovely word for this glorious return of the swans.

Swanfall it is called, because the birds seem almost to drop from the sky once they reach their wintering grounds. Swanfall. To the scientists it was an event to be celebrated, like the turning of color in the autumn leaves, or the opening of the cherry blossoms each spring in Washington, DC—a time to appreciate nature's poetry.

Other eyes appreciated the swanfall too. The huge birds stirred different emotions in the heart of a teenage boy whose father raised grain on fields bordering the bay shore in Virginia. It had been many decades since tundra swans were hunted in the bay region.

Recently their populations had been growing, to nearly one hundred thousand wintering in the eastern United States, and about eighty thousand migrating down the West Coast to California. Pressure to hunt them had arisen. Biologically there was no reason not to, said the game managers. The swans' numbers were large enough that a controlled portion could be "cropped" without any threat to their survival as a species.

The scientist, who thought of the swans as poets and musicians and as creatures with tight family bonds, found such thinking chilling and argued against a hunt. But the state decided to open the season on a limited basis. The farm boy read an exciting article in a shooting magazine that described the tundra swan as the ultimate trophy for a waterfowler. He was determined to possess one of these magnificent creatures, to bring one down to be skinned and stuffed, mounted and admired.

Even in the days a century before, when unregulated baiting and hunting took tremendous tolls on the nation's waterfowl, it had not been an easy thing to kill a tundra swan. They are among the wariest of the waterfowl.

The approach of an oysterman's vessel within more than several hundred yards caused the male and female to begin paddling rapidly, keeping a margin of safety between their brood and the boat. And though the swans rooted close to the marsh banks for soft clams and the nutritious root systems of wigeon grass and eelgrass, one of the adults was always on the lookout for the slightest movement of a raccoon, a fox, or a human.

However, the lull of recent decades in shooting swans on the Chesapeake had somewhat blunted millions of years of instinctive caution in the adult swans, who now fed with their three cygnets in a quiet cove south of the Blackwater Refuge, near the Maryland-Virginia state line.

As long as they remained on the water, the swans were relatively safe from predators, human and otherwise. For thousands of years the rich aquatic life in the bay's shallows had been sufficient to feed the swans each winter. But in recent years human activities on the lands that drain into the great bay had caused an environmental disaster below the surface.

The farmers now grew more and more corn and soybeans, and for years they had been applying greater amounts of fertilizer to these crops to boost yields. The fertilizers washed into the bay, fueling the growth of tiny floating plant life called algae.

So much algae now grew that it clouded the water, cutting off light that the submerged vegetation, the swans' traditional food, needed to grow. At the same time, growing human populations also sent more and more sewage into the bay, with the same effect of increasing the growth of algae. The combination of agriculture and sewage had overwhelmed the natural system. In less than a decade, the grasses, for the first time in history, nearly vanished across hundreds of thousands of acres of the Chesapeake Bay. Efforts to bring them back were under way, but a recovery would be many years ahead, if it came at all.

Some species of waterfowl adapted. On the bay, and on Lake Erie, where the same thing had happened a decade earlier, the swans switched almost overnight from feeding on vegetation to flying far inland to forage in fields.

Many other species, like the redhead and wigeon ducks that had dined on the debris uprooted by feeding swans, could not adapt, and very few of them now remained.

So it was that one December morning found the two adults leading their three cygnets away from the isolation of their traditional coves to spend the day amid fields of grain stubble and tender shoots of winter wheat. Many farmers cursed at this invasion, little thinking how they had helped to cause it.

The days were short now, and as the swan family winged back to the water's safety, long shadows flowed

swiftly across the land. They obscured the outlines of a rough blind constructed of brush and reeds where a line of dark cedars grew almost to the marshy shore edge. The swans flew low as they crossed the shore. The wild geese, hunted heavily, had learned never to drop low in flight until they were well out over water.

The boy sat inside the blind, motionless, on an upturned crab basket, shotgun at the ready. He loved the bay in all seasons, loved to dip the soft-shell crab from the summer marsh, to stalk the shallows in winter for a mess of fat oysters, to fall asleep at night to the wintry grace notes of the geese and swans floating from the creek near his family's farm.

He had sat many days in the blind from sunrise to sunset and gone home empty-handed but filled with the sheer beauty of the day and the bay. Yet, even on such days, it was the kill, or the possibility of it, that heightened all his senses and made the waiting somehow more satisfying than if he'd had only a pair of binoculars by his side.

In years to come, as the boy grew old, the beauty of waterfowl would come to mean more, and the killing of them less; but just now, crouched low, heart pounding to the whistling wing beats of approaching swans, he was predator, they were prey. All other thought was banished by that.

The male, attracted by the boy's artful arrangement of decoys on the water, swung his little family lower, but still out of shotgun range. Perhaps it was a feeding place. They would circle again for a closer look. But the cygnets had no such caution or patience. Peeling from formation, they set their wings for a landing straight into the decoys. The boy rose to meet them.

Too late the trio realized that something was terribly amiss. Fire flashed amid a thunderous peal from the black shadows of the cedars. A cygnet crumpled in midair, the life force that had propelled it here across four thousand miles gone before it splatted limply on the water's surface.

Laboring frantically to regain altitude, its two siblings seemed to hang motionless before the boy's gunsight. That was his youthful mistake. Despite their slow wing beats, the birds were moving several feet a second by now. His last two shots tore the air harmlessly several feet behind the cygnets.

The swans quickly receded into the sun's afterglow on the western horizon. The stars were beginning to peep out as the boy gathered his decoys and his kill.

Far out on the bay, the familiar *wow-HOW-oo*'s had started up for another night.

December slipped into January and February. The swans settled into a routine of feeding and resting. For such long-distance flyers, they ranged surprisingly short distances on the bay. The marsh cove where the two adults and their remaining cygnets wintered was the same spot to which the male and female had been returning since they first mated, seven years earlier. For all their lordly appearance and globe-girdling abilities, the tundra swans were small-town folks at heart.

Some days fierce storms hurled snow and ice across the Chesapeake, and the swans would huddle for protection under the lee shores of the marsh, not feeding for days, until the danger was past. Only the heat generated by their great, insulated bodies kept ice from forming across the coves. If ice grew solid, foxes and raccoons on the shore would take quick advantage of such a bridge. The swans' stores of fat, which had made up a quarter of their body weight at the time of swanfall, would shrink to less than 10 percent before winter ended.

Often there would come a fine day, even in the deepest winter, when the sun shone warm and hazy and the waters of the Chesapeake lay smooth as slate. Then the swans with their extended families would gather and flip on their backs, abandoning all pretense of grace and majesty. Legs kicking the air, wings flailing, the great fowl frolicked with all the abandon of children in a snowdrift.

Who is to say whether birds and animals do not sometimes just do things for fun? Certainly the swans seemed to revel in this "Saturday night bath." But there was also common sense to their ritual. As they romped, they *preened,* pressing with their bills on a gland near their tails. This gland secreted oil that the birds spread throughout their feathers, renewing their waterproofing and repairing tears in their all-important insulation.

The days, which reach their shortest point in the Northern Hemisphere just before Christmas, began to lengthen noticeably as January and February slipped into early March. The Chesapeake was at its emptiest. Oystering had ended, and crabbing had not yet begun. Hunting season was over, and the water had not yet warmed enough for most fishing. The Canada geese had departed for their breeding grounds in Labrador, and many of the ducks were already winging toward their Canadian prairie nesting places.

All threats of ice were gone, and daytime temperatures were mild. It seemed the laziest of times for the swans, but they were already beginning a critical race with the seasons. The male and female grew more and more restless now, scanning the skies, necks extended, *how-ooo*ing back and forth to other swan families day and night, raising a din like a pack of hounds on the scent of game.

They preened constantly, and courtship had begun. The adults kept more distance from their cygnets these days. They often faced each other, bobbing their heads up and down, the motions at first independent of each other, then merging into perfect synchrony. Then, breasts almost touching, necks thrust out, wings extended, both would join in piercing calls that carried for miles across the bay waters.

These displays were repeated often, each repetition bonding the pair more firmly. They would remain joined as long as both lived. It is a trait that humans find heartwarming, a good example for themselves. But the lifelong allegiance of the swans to each other most likely has a quite practical reason. The Arctic summer allows precious little time for birds of their size to nest and ready their young for migrating. The same experienced and familiar pair of adults year after year is more likely to meet the harsh deadlines of the northern tundra for successfully reproducing than birds who must work at new relationships every year.

One day in mid-March, the angle of the sun, or perhaps the growing length of daylight, triggered something deep in the swans' ancestral memories. It was time to be leaving.

The sounds of their taking off, wing tips clop-clopping on the water, echoed across the marshes like

the chop of waves against the bank. A thousand *wow-HOW-ooo*'s joined together. Then it was quiet. The bay had lost its wildest voice until swanfall again came round.

The flocks this time moved less than a hundred miles, passing over Baltimore and setting down near Washington Boro, on the Susquehanna River in Pennsylvania. On the swans' northward migration, there was no major weather front boosting their flight, nor quite the epic journey of the previous fall. They moved in shorter hops, pausing on Lake Erie and at marshes along the upper Mississippi River, hopping through central Canada and the great Mackenzie River delta. Nowhere did they stop long, because there was no time to waste.

It is May, full spring back on the Chesapeake, but the tundra on Alaska's North Slope looks nearly the same as it does in the dead of winter. The male and female swan fly now along the slope of Alaska's mighty Brooks Range, a jumble of peaks as sharp and white as whipped meringue. They descend over a treeless, frozen plain, stretching away to the frozen Arctic Ocean.

The Eskimos have a saying about this land where the eye strains to find the horizons. They say no matter how far or fast you travel, the place where the land

and the sky join will always be stretching far ahead. Maybe that is why the caribou migrate in their great herds every year, the natives say—running, always running, looking for a home where the earth and sky finally merge.

Even in this featureless world of white, the swans gleam almost incandescent in the clear arctic daylight as they wheel over the tundra toward a familiar lake. Wherever they go, they are always the brightest objects in their realm.

Many adult pairs are without their cygnets now or are expelling them from the immediate family. It is at first a painful separation. For a year, the young have never been out of their parents' sight, seldom more than a few yards from them.

Here on the North Slope, the cygnets will join other immature adults for the summer. It will be two more years before they mature, perhaps four years before they take mates.

It has been a snowy winter on the North Slope. This is unusual because the arctic tundra is nearly a desert. Less than ten inches of precipitation fall here annually, an average comparable to much of Nevada.

Only the permafrost maintains the shallow lakes and ponds that support the tundra swans through the summer. The soil underlying the tundra never thaws, forming a layer that the rainfall and melting snow cannot soak through.

On the ground, the swans fret about, plucking at the roots of submerged grasses on the edges of a few thawing ponds. Their nest, the same one they have returned to each year, is still under snow. This is a bad omen, for the swans' race with the brief arctic summer has now begun in earnest.

It takes a full month for the female, once she lays her eggs, to incubate them to hatching. Another two months will pass before the cygnets can make their first, stumbling flights. By then, only days will be left before advancing winter forces the birds once again on the long migration.

Daily the snow melts. The female feeds heavily in the ponds and marsh, storing food reserves for egg laying. The male works at rebuilding the old nest from nearby vegetation until it rises nearly three feet off the tundra. The resulting structure is a small island surrounded by water and marsh, easy to guard against the arctic foxes and the wolves that are patrolling the thawing tundra, hungry for prey.

The male also begins to reestablish his breeding territory, making constant flights outward from the nest across the surrounding tundra, blaring, trumpet-

like, his warning to any creature that dares to move through his area of half a mile square or more.

An observer who visited these breeding grounds expecting to see spectacular gatherings of swans would be hardpressed to find more than a few dozen of the birds in a day's travel on foot, so scattered are they in their huge individual nesting territories. Even by plane, one must sometimes travel a few minutes between breeding pairs.

It is mid-June before four creamy white eggs, four times the size of a chicken egg and equally rounded at each end, fill the nest. The female seldom leaves it for long now. Frequently she drips water from her bill over the eggs to maintain their inner moisture. The male patrols the boundaries of their territory.

One morning another swan, a subadult hatched two years before, arrows across the invisible boundaries, attracted by a pond lined with succulent grasses.

Too late, he hears the big male's yelp and turns his neck in flight to see the older swan closing fast, neck extended like some righteous, white spear. Fleeing for his life, the young adult hears the whistle of beating wings and feels a beak clamp on his rump feathers.

Rudely, he is jerked backward and down, crashing to the earth thirty-feet below and bouncing off the tundra. The plunge knocks the breath from his lungs. The light is blotted out by the avenging presence of his attacker, hovering over the bruised swan, clubbing him mercilessly with the knobby "wrist" bones of wings that span seven feet.

Battered almost senseless, the young swan drags himself far enough away to appease the hissing male momentarily and regain the air. He will not intrude again.

The male returns to the nest, where his mate joins him in a victory ritual. Facing, breast to breast, beaks extended skyward, they bugle a duet while beating their outstretched wings together. Repeated several times during the summer, this display serves as a warning to the whole tundra and further bonds the swans to each other and to their territory.

The eggs hatch in late July—later than is ideal. Only in the last few weeks has full summer come to the tundra, flushing the landscape a greenish brown and splashing it with unaccustomed color—the lemony yellows and purples of saxifrage and the puffy white mounds of cotton grass. Sunlight now lasts nearly twenty-four hours at these northern latitudes.

A grizzly bear and her cub amble near the swans, seeming uninterested in the birds or the male's aggressive posturing. Golden eagles and gulls circle above, a constant threat; they will swoop down on eggs and young cygnets if a nest is left unguarded.

As soon as their silvery gray fuzz has dried beneath the wings of their mother, the cygnets begin feeding on their own. At first they peck clumsily at small pieces of submerged vegetation churned up by the feeding adults, and stab, with mixed success, at insects on the surface of the ponds. They must grow from several ounces to more than ten pounds in the next seven or eight weeks and gain strength enough, at only a few months of age, to fly thousands of miles.

The compressed arctic seasons fly by as the family of swans bask in the long daylight. The first sunset since June comes on August 4, but darkness lasts only two hours. Already temperatures are dipping below freezing in the twilight evenings.

One day the swans feel the earth beneath their feet trembling. A family of wolves lope by, eyes and noses fixed on a long brown line quivering along the horizon. Soon a river of shaggy, great-antlered caribou, part of Alaska's Porcupine herd, is pouring across the tundra. Like the swans, they follow ancient routes each year, prodded on their way by the weather and the seasons.

The landscape now is daubed with the hues of late autumn. The sedges are yellowing, and the bearberries and arctophila, a marsh plant, glow a crimson brilliant as any New England maple. A snow squall blows in one day off the ocean, where ice floes dot the blue-green waters. Each morning ice skims the smallest ponds, fragile as a windowpane. The adults easily break through it to feed.

As September advances, the sky is filled some mornings with the ringing notes of young and unmated swans departing for the Dakotas. The male and female show their old, familiar restlessness as the days grow shorter by nearly an hour each week.

Two of the cygnets test their wings frequently, flapping and hopping to the accompaniment of high-pitched *wheep-wheep*ing. The third one, smaller than his sisters, lags behind. The ice grows each morning. The swans stand on the smaller ponds now.

One morning the male cocks his head and stands without moving for more than a minute. No sound fixes his attention. Rather he may sense the subtle dropping of barometric pressure that means a big winter storm is on its way. That afternoon the family takes wing. The third cygnet flaps furiously, wheeping piteously, but he is still days from flying, and the days have run out.

The family circles once, necks craning down toward the lone cygnet, *how-ooo*ing encouragement, or maybe farewell.

The unforgiving timetable that dictates the cycles of the tundra swan means the cygnet will not survive the night. But it also means that his species will survive long, and the glad tidings of swanfall will complete the Chesapeake autumn for many centuries to come.